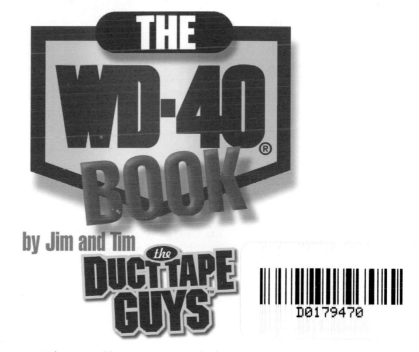

THE
WD-40 ®
BOOK

by Jim and Tim the DUCT TAPE GUYS™

D0179470

Adventure Publications, Inc.   Cambridge, Minnesota

Adventure Publications in conjunction with The Duct Tape Guys and Octane Creative

World Wide Web: http://www.ducttapeguys.com

The WD-40® Book by Jim and Tim–The Duct Tape Guys™

Printed in the United States of America.
02 03 04 05 06 07   10 9 8 7 6 5 4

Text: Tony Dierckins and Tim Nyberg, with assist and inspiration by Jim Berg
Illustrations and photo alteration: Tim Nyberg. Photography: Erik Saulitis, and MetaPhotos.

Retail distribution:
Adventure Publications 800-678-7006 / 820 Cleveland Street South, Cambridge, MN 55008
Specialty distribution and reprint permission:
Octane Creative 800-270-5863 / P.O. Box 130066, Roseville, MN 55113, USA

ISBN 1-887317-15-5
Library of Congress Catalog Card Number: 97-70677

Warning: Contains humor, a highly volatile substance if used improperly. Harmful if swallowed. All content is a fictional product of the authors' imaginations. Any resemblance between characters portrayed herein and actual persons living, dead, or residing in New Jersey is purely coincidental. Contents under pressure. Do not use near open flame. Do not use as a flotation device, or at least avoid any situations in which you would need to rely on a book as a flotation device. Any typographic errors are purely intentional and left for your amusement. Always say no to drugs and, by all means, stay in school. Read further warnings on the next page and pages 72 and 73.

WARNING!

The uses of WD-40 spray lubricant described in this **humor book** do not constitute recommendations or suggestions for use of WD-40 spray lubricant by either WD-40 Company, Bad Dog Press, or the authors. *Consumers should always and only follow the instructions and take heed of any warnings printed on the WD-40 spray lubricant packaging.*

See pages 72 and 73 for complete warnings.

Introduction

Jim & Tim's Introduction:

Hey! We wrote us another book!

Editor's Introduction:

Fans of Jim & Tim are already familiar with their *Duct Tape* books and calendars, handy little guides to the myriad of uses for America's favorite adhesive. But Jim & Tim are hardly simpletons who have dedicated their lives to spreading the gospel of duct tape. No, they're complex individuals who also enjoy the peacc of mind that comes with knowing the value of a handy can of WD-40. Like duct tape, this product has many, many uses.

Officially, WD-40 Company will tell you that its namesake product does only five things: lubricates, cleans, protects, penetrates, and displaces moisture.

Well, we all know full well that it does much more than that. For years, thousands of Americans have been sending WD-40 Company testimonial letters describing their unique uses for this little miracle in a blue-and-yellow can. We've compiled some of the very best, most unique uses in this volume, and Jim & Tim have graciously contributed some of the countless ways they have found WD-40 useful over the years. (And as if that wasn't enough, there's also a whole appendix in the back filled with even *more* WD-40 ideas from other testimonial letters.)

Now, do be careful: Jim & Tim are professionals with big, expensive life and health insurance policies. We at Bad Dog Press recommend that you do not try their ideas unless you're in the presence of a paramedic, a trained physician or veterinarian, or a semiprofessional bowler.

Enjoy the book, spray safely, and remember the wisdom of the authors, Jim & Tim, The Duct Tape Guys:

"If it's not stuck and it's supposed to be—duct tape it! If it's stuck and it's not supposed to be, WD-40 it!"

— The Editors of Bad Dog Press (1997)

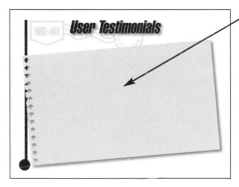

Each left-hand page features an actual "User Testimonial" tip sent in by WD-40 enthusiasts everywhere.

— *And sometimes Jim and me will add a variation on the tip or say somethin' clever.*

— *That's right, Tim. And you'll know it's us 'cause all the stuff we say is in italics.*

— *And we're not even Italian.*

— *Oh, yeah. Good point.*

On the right-hand pages, we share the way WE use WD-40 to make our lives better.

— *Not that readers should try our ideas.*

— *No way. We're professionals.*

— *And we're not even Italian.*

— *Oh, yeah. Good, uh.... Good... I don't know what that means.*

— *Well, it.... It sounded good last time.*

Removes super strong glue from fingers and other unwanted surfaces.

— *Super strong glue? Why would you even need Super strong glue with duct tape in your tool box, Jim?*

— *Why would anyone willingly marry Michael Jackson? It's just one of life's great mysteries, Tim.*

2

Removes unwanted fingers from cookie jars, purses, wallets, and your personal stash of duct tape and WD-40.

*Wisdom subject to change without notice.

3

Car owners with leaky oil pans:
Spray on concrete driveways
to remove unsightly
oil spots.

Homeowners with annoying neighbors: Spray on neighbors' property to avoid the build-up of unsightly junk cars.

Softens and preserves
leather furniture.

6

Makes your old vinyl
car seats look like new.

— *Yeah, but you better buckle up.*

— *I said I was sorry, Tim.*

— *I almost slid right through
the windshield.*

7

WD-40 was used to free a boy whose arm was stuck up to his shoulder in a sewer.

Does your kid keep getting his head stuck in iron gate railings? Don't send him out to play without a preventive squirt behind each ear.

*Wisdom subject to change without notice.

9

Keeps grandfather clocks lubricated and running smooth.

Keeps grandfathers lubricated and running smooth.

— *Um, Tim, I'm pretty sure it's that stuff Grandpa keeps sippin' from that Mason jar that keeps him lubricated.*

*Wisdom subject to change without notice.

11

Spray on your car's hoses and fan belts to prevent them from drying out and cracking.

Overcook and dry out the Thanksgiving turkey? Spray it down with—

— *Wait a minute, Tim. You can't spray WD-40 on food.*

— *Why not?*

— *Because, stupid: WD-40 is a petroleum product. You can't swallow petroleum products.*

— *Have you ever had my wife's turkey? You can't hardly swallow that, either.*

Spray on new shoes to soften them up—makes them more comfortable and prevents blisters.

Spray on toads before you handle them—prevents warts.

— *That's an old wives' tale, Jim.*

— *Oh, right. Spray it on old wives' tails to prevent warts.*

— *That's better.*

Motorists:
Spray on the front of your car to
avoid build-up of squished bugs
on the grill.

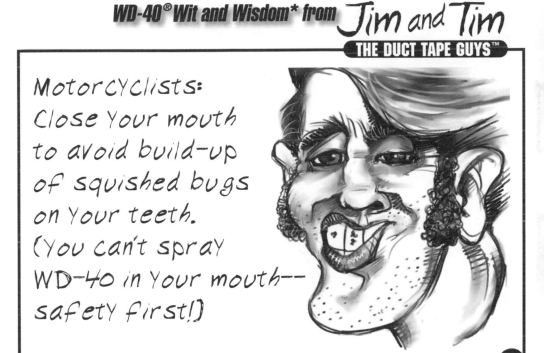

Motorcyclists:
Close Your mouth
to avoid build-up
of squished bugs
on Your teeth.
(You can't spray
WD-40 in Your mouth—
safety first!)

*Wisdom subject to change without notice.

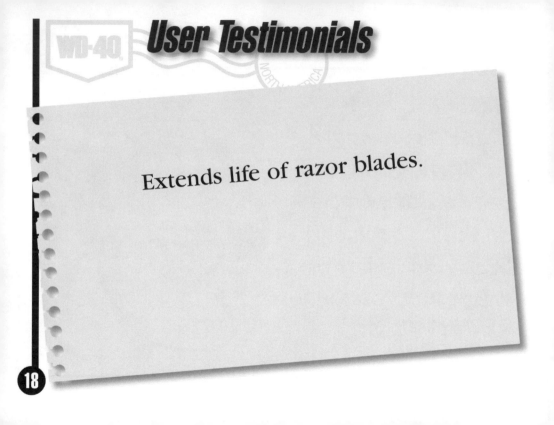

Extends life of razor blades.

Run out of shaving cream?
WD-40 makes a great substitute!

— *Yeah, just be careful—less friction means a faster, potentially more dangerous shave.*

— *Yeah, you had a whole roll of toilet paper stuck to your face for a week.*

— *Shut up, Jim.*

— *You could've used a styptic pencil the size of a telephone pole.*

— *I said shut up, Jim!*

*Wisdom subject to change without notice.

19

Spray on box-spring mattresses to remove squeak and avoid embarrassing looks from the downstairs neighbors.

*Wisdom subject to change without notice.

Shines your mother-of-pearl accessories.

Shines your
mother-in-law.

— *Fat-lot of good that did, Tim.*

— *I said I was sorry.*

— *Well, once again you ruined Christmas for everyone.*

23

the History of WD-40

America, 1953. The sound barrier has just been broken, the aerospace industry is booming. In San Diego, California, tiny Rocket Chemical—a fledgling company with a staff of three—sets out to create a rust-preventive solvent that can displace water.

After forty attempts to develop this water-displacing solvent, the work of founder Norm Larson and his compatriots at Rocket Chemical pays off. WD-40®—Water Displacer perfected on the fortieth try—is born. Yet it won't be until 1958, a full five years after its birth, that WD-40 will be packaged in the familiar blue-and-yellow spray can America knows and loves today. The rest, as they say, is history.

Well, at least that's what WD-40 Company will tell you.

Let's backtrack: America, 1953. America likes Ike and his Commie-bashing running mate, Dick Nixon; on a disturbing note, Oppenheimer unleashes the power of the hydrogen bomb; on an even more disturbing note "comedienne" Roseanne's parents unleash Roseanne; and finally, "The Adventures of Ozzie & Harriet" entertain us and provide us with a role model for life in the carefree fifties, made even more carefree for us Americans as the miracle of duct tape—developed during World War II—quietly sweeps across a restless nation as an integral part of its postwar housing boom.

Yes, duct tape. America had television, was about to get rock-n-roll, and enjoyed the peace that comes with the ability to destroy any industrialized nation that dared challenge it. It needed something to make things stuck that needed to be stuck, and duct tape was that thing. But what about when things were stuck that shouldn't be stuck? What then? What could they use?

Flash forward: 1957. The scene: a kitchen in a simple house in San Diego. A frustrated housewife—lacking sufficient household products due to financial concerns as her husband's company, Rocket Chemical, struggles to sell its water-displacer outside the aerospace industry—tries in vain to keep house efficiently. No cleaning products, floor waxes, or furniture polish at hand; nothing to quiet squeaks or loosen stubborn bolts as she works on the family Edsel. She spies a jar of her husband's product on the countertop, puts a little

on an old rag, and uses it to polish the blond oak furniture in the living room. Coffee stains disappear and the wood glows, but when she sets the over-sized ashtray back down on the unlevel coffee table, the ceramic, glass-bead-encrusted ash receptacle slides right off, and a thought occurs to her: *This stuff makes things like new—and slippery, too. I wonder what else it's good for?*

"If this stuff came in a spray can," Mrs. Larson tells her husband later that day, "I'd buy it by the case."

And so he put it in a spray can—a blue-and-yellow spray can to match his wife's kitchen—and soon realized he'd created a companion product to America's favorite adhesive, a handy spray lubricant that—like duct tape—has a myriad of uses beyond what it was intended for.

God bless us, everyone.

Cobblers:
Waterproofs, shines, and softens
leather shoes.

Removes cat paw marks from furniture and the hood of your car.

Spray on your furniture and car to keep cats from walking on your stuff in the first place.

31

*Wisdom subject to change without notice.

Lubricates playground equipment—swings, teeter-totters, slides, etc.

Spray down your kids' backsides so they don't stick to those hot metal playground slides. Turns "Yikes!" into "Wheeee!"

Wisdom subject to change without notice.

Keeps snow from sticking
to snow shovels.

Spray down the sidewalk and driveway and you'll never have to shovel again!

— *But watch your step.*

— *Yeah, and you may want to warn your postal carrier, too. No mail for two months.*

— *It was your idea, Jim.*

*Wisdom subject to change without notice.

Prevents squirrels from climbing the bird-feeder pole.

Prevents your dog from climbing on visitors' legs.

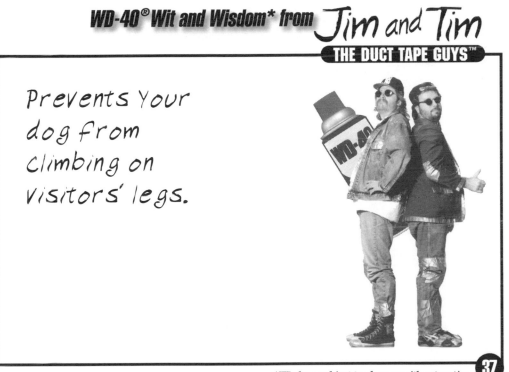

*Wisdom subject to change without notice.

37

Housekeepers:
Spray on floor for that
just-waxed sheen.

Bodybuilders:
Spray on body for that
just pumped-up sheen.

*Wisdom subject to change without notice.

Spray on sled runners to
keep them free
from snow build-up.

Spray on sledders
to keep them free
from the need of a sled.

*Wisdom subject to change without notice.

41

Guitarists' best friend:
Cleans and lubricates guitar strings.

— *Gives new meaning to the term "slide guitar."*

— *Good one, Tim.*

Road managers' best friend: Cleans up overlubricated guitar players.

*Wisdom subject to change without notice.

Spray on wooden outhouse toilet seat to prevent the wood from drying out, cracking, and causing painful splinters.

Spray on toilet seat to prevent hemorrhoids caused by prolonged sitting (it's hard to read the newspaper when you're sliding off the seat).

Shoppers: Stuck with a wobbly, sticky-wheeled shopping cart? Spray wheels with WD-40 to reduce wobbling and friction—less friction means faster shopping!

Shutterbugs: Stuck with slow 200-speed film after running out of 400-speed film? Spray the 200-speed film with WD-40--less friction means faster film!

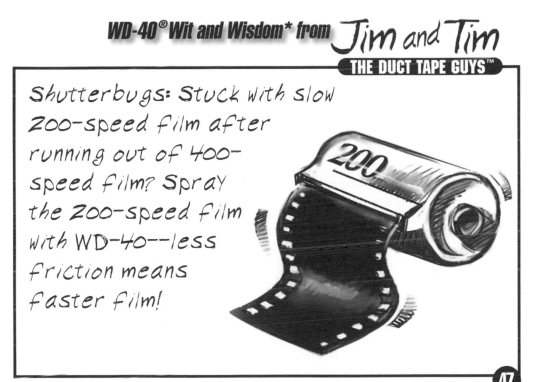

*Wisdom subject to change without notice.

Removes gum from hair and a variety of surfaces.

Removes hair from gum for continued chewing pleasure.

*Wisdom subject to change without notice.

Spin-off Products

Jim & Tim's WD-40 Spin-off Product Ideas*

As avid users of WD-40, Jim and Tim have developed product ideas and submitted them to the WD-40 Company, hoping that the manufacturer of their favorite spray lubricant would turn their ideas into marketable products, share the profits, and allow Jim and Tim to keep themselves in duct tape and WD-40 for life. Sadly, not a single one of the boys' ideas has developed into anything but kindly phrased rejection letters. We at Bad Dog Press, however, think their ideas are worth sharing:

- **"WD-Pourri"** (Scented WD-40)

  Since WD-40 covers up unwanted odors, the boys thought they could tap into a whole new market by making WD-40 available in a variety of scents, including pine, lemon-fresh, new car, potpourri, and just-ripped duct tape. The letter from WD-40 Company mentioned something about "low consumer need."

*That were flat-out rejected outright by WD-40 Company

- **"SPRAM"** *(WD-40's Nonstick, No-Calorie Cooking Spray)**

  The boys were heartbroken when they received the "No Thank You" note from the WD-40 Company and when they first saw a commercial for PAM™ Cooking Spray. To date, they have received no reply to their "We told you so" letter.

- **"I Can't Believe It's Not WD-40"** *(Fat-Free, Butter-Flavored WD-40)**

  A spin-off of their "SPRAM" idea, Jim and Tim thought they had a winner here, but our heroes came up against a bigger obstacle than corporate naysayers—the Food and Drug Administration.

- **"Spert Plus"** *(WD-40 Shower-Free Shampoo-and-Conditioner-in-One—With Aloe!)*

  Even the convenience of a spray-on, all-purpose hair-care product that works without the hassle of bathing wasn't enough for the WD-40 Company to venture into the limitless potential of this product, but Jim & Tim continue to use their favorite spray lubricant despite their barber's complaints that his scissors keeps slipping.

*Although they may sound like the work of genius, don't try your own variations of Jim & Tim's ideas: WD-40 is a petroleum product and should never be ingested.

Lubricates chain-saw chains.

Lubricates lumberjacks.

— *Lumberjacks?*

— *Yeah, like in* The Wizard of Oz. *The Duct Tape Lumberjack came to life with WD-40.*

— *Um... That was the Tin Man. And it was oil. He had an oil can.*

— *Oh... Oh, yeah. Sorry.*

*Wisdom subject to change without notice.

Wintertime tip:
Spray on leather and suede shoes
and boots to prevent water and salt
staining, or spray on salt-stained boots
to remove the stains.

Party-time-tip:
Avoid spraying
WD-40 on the rim
of your Margarita
and Bloody Mary
glasses or you'll
never get the salt
to stick to the rim!

Wisdom subject to change without notice.

55

Unfreeze frozen car door locks, or put an end to frozen car door locks with a preventive squirt when it gets real cold.

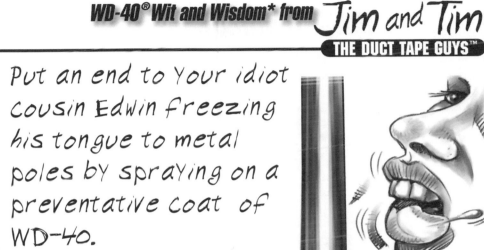

Put an end to Your idiot cousin Edwin freezing his tongue to metal poles by spraying on a preventative coat of WD-40.

— *On the pole, or on Cousin Edwin's tongue?*

— *The pole, stupid! Never spray WD-40 in someone's mouth!*

57

Prevents cracks in
rubber garden hose.

Or maybe prevent wisecracks from your know-it-all brother-in-law.

— *Oh yeah?*

— *Yeah.*

— *Yeah, well—so there.*

— *Oh, yeah—good one.*

*Wisdom subject to change without notice.

Golfers:
WD-40 cleans and protects golf clubs
and helps loosen stuck-on spikes.

Golfers:

WD-40 can improve your game!

Spray on tees and balls:

Less friction =

more velocity =

longer tee shots!

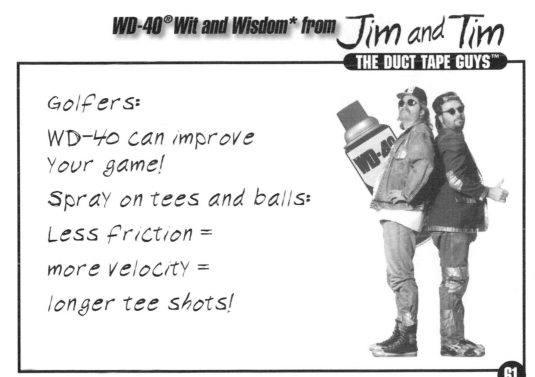

Works as a spot remover/pre-treater on stubborn stains—even those tough blood stains.

— *Hey, if you have a chronic problem with blood stains, I'm thinkin' you've got more to worry about than laundry problems.*

— *Yeah, right.*

Sloppy eaters: Anticipate food stain problems and spray your entire outfit. Food will slide right off.

*Wisdom subject to change without notice.

Spray perimeter of garden to keep neighbor's annoying dogs away from your flower bed.

Spray on perimeter
of house to keep
neighbor's annoying son
away from your
daughter.

*Wisdom subject to change without notice.

Keeps flies off cows.

Keeps
cows off
barns.

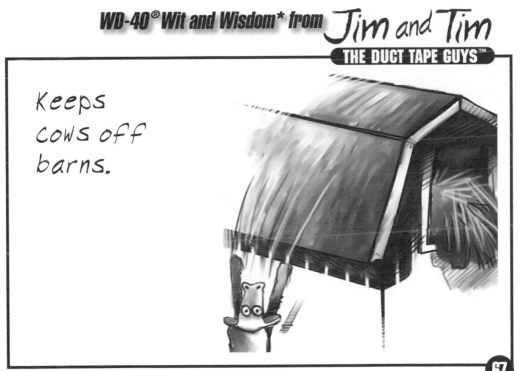

*Wisdom subject to change without notice.

67

Perfect for the garden shed:
WD-40 cleans and reconditions your
metal gardening tools, leaving behind a
protective film that prevents
rust and corrossion.

Perfect for the shower: cleans and conditions your hair, restoring body as it prevents hair rust and corrosion.

69

*Wisdom subject to change without notice.

Prevents wasps from
building nests on your house.

Prevents WASPS from building
houses near Your nest.

— *I don't get it, Jim.*

— *WASPS: White Anglo-Saxon Protestants.*

— *Why don't we want 'em building houses by ours?
Isn't that racist?*

— *Well, maybe, Tim. But it's funny, and they're a majority,
so it's kinda OK to do it.*

— *But if they're a majority, aren't a lot of them going to buy
this book?*

— *Oh, yeah. Hey, sorry all you WASPS, er, Pigment-Challenged
Americans.*

WD-40 Safety Tips

While WD-40 has a myriad of uses that go well beyond the tasks it was originally designed to perform, users should always be careful when using it in certain circumstances.

Keep the following guidelines in mind as you safely spray your worries away:

- DO NOT USE WD-40 NEAR HEAT SOURCES (keep spray away from heat, sparks, pilot lights, open flame; disconnect electrical tools and appliances before spraying.)
- DO NOT USE WD-40 NEAR ELECTRICAL CURRENTS OR BATTERY TERMINALS (electrical arcing can cause burn-through [puncture], which may result in flash fire).
- DO NOT PLACE WD-40 ON HOT SURFACES OR IN DIRECT SUNLIGHT (heat may cause bursting).
- DO NOT SWALLOW WD-40 (contains petroleum distillates; if swallowed DO NOT induce vomiting; call a physician immediately).
- DO NOT INHALE WD-40 (deliberate or direct inhalation of vapor or spray mist may be harmful or fatal).
- DO NOT STORE ABOVE 120°F OR DAMAGE CAN (contents under pressure; do not puncture, crush, or incinerate [burn] can, even when emptied).

WD-40 FIRST AID:
- Ingestion (swallowed): Seek medical attention.
- Eye Contact: Immediately flush eye with large amounts of water for 15 minutes.
- Skin contact: Wash with soap and water.
- Inhalation (breathing): Remove to fresh air; give artificial respiration or oxygen if necessary.

JIM & TIM'S WD-40 SAFETY TIPS:

As avid users of WD-40, Jim and Tim have used this wonderful product to help them whenever it seemed appropriate. Unfortunately, not everything they've asked the product to do has worked out as they expected. The following list of dos and don'ts is based on their experience:

- NEVER use WD-40 to clean your contact lenses.
- NEVER use WD-40 as a nasal decongestant.
- NEVER use WD-40 to clean your ear canal.
- Using WD-40 on your steps and sidewalk may rid them of ice, but it will NOT make the surface less slippery.
- While WD-40 acts as a degreaser, keep in mind that spraying it on your food will not make it "fat-free" and may have some effect on taste.
- We should also point out that there is no actual funded research *recognized* by the AMA backing up any claims that bathing in WD-40 will help you clear up your skin, lose weight, quit smoking, send cancer cells into remission, find the perfect mate, or stop telemarketers from phoning during dinner.

Prevent—and get rid of—fleas and ticks from infesting your dog: Spray Fido with WD-40 before he goes outside.*

(Also cures mange on dogs.)

*But never spray near a dog's eyes, nose, or mouth!

Prevent wet dog smell: Spray Fido with WD-40 before you let him out when it's raining. (This will also prevent him from rolling in dead animals and other icky stuff. He'll slide right off!)

*Wisdom subject to change without notice.

Spray on bait and lures
to attract fish.

Spray on pulse points to attract a mate.

— *And if your car breaks down on the highway and you're out of duct tape, you can spray it in the air to attract a mechanic.*

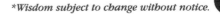

77

Removes rust from
(and prevents rust from forming on)
a variety of surfaces.

Removes teenage daughter's face from, and prevents her face from becoming adhered to, the telephone.

*Wisdom subject to change without notice.

Degreases engine blocks and other automotive parts.

Degreases hair of overzealous Bryl Creem™ users.

— *Hey, Jim: I wonder how it would work on Jerry Lewis's head.*

— *Nothing's THAT strong, Tim.*

Neatnik teachers:
Restores and cleans chalkboards.

Naughty students:

Spray on chalk and chalkboards to write "I will not compare the teacher's disciplinary methods with fascism" 100 times in no time!

83

Removes paint, grease, caulking, paneling glue, tar, and pine pitch from your hands.

Removes hands of
overaggressive date
from You.

Lost your pine tree air freshener?
Masks unpleasant odors
inside car.

Run out of deodorant?
Masks unpleasant
odors under arms.

— *Or under your brother-in-law.*

— *Shut up, Jim.*

87

*Wisdom subject to change without notice.

Entrants in Pasadena's Tournament of Roses Parade reportedly spray down their floats to keep moisture off the flowers and mechanisms whenever it literally rains on their parade.

Caught in the rain at the bus stop? Borrow a newspaper, fold it into a paper hat, and spray it with WD-40. Instant rain bonnet!

*Wisdom subject to change without notice.

89

Helps break in new baseball
and softball gloves.

— *Don't forget to wipe off the excess WD-40 before you play.*

— *I said I was sorry, Jim.*

— *Cost us the championship, Mr. "WD-40 Fingers."*

Pitchers: improve Your earned run average with a squirt or two in Your glove; use it to lube up Your fingers and the ball and soon You'll be throwing the ultimate slider.

*Wisdom subject to change without notice.

Removes lipstick stains.

Removes your over-affectionate aunt's lips from your face:

Spray a little WD-40 into your hands and apply to your cheeks; when your aunt pinches you, her fingers will slide right off and she won't even think of plantin' one on ya.

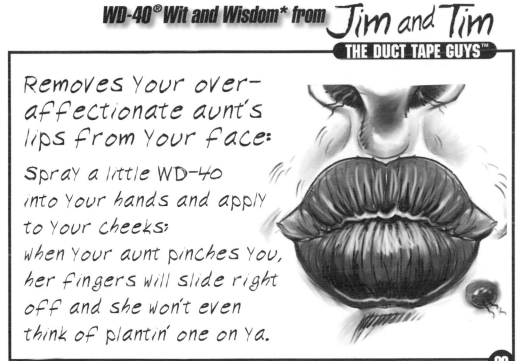

93

Unsticks keys on computer keyboards.

94

Unsticks computer geeks from computer keyboards even after they've spent hours on-line in chat rooms discussing their favorite episodes of "Star Trek."

Rejuvenates sticky computer mouse.

— Hey, Tim: Couldn't you spray it into the computer to stop it from "freezing up."

— Well, maybe. But it might also wreck your whole computer.

— Oh, yeah. Better not do that.

Rejuvenates icky lab rat.

97

Removes old wax from skis
and snowboards
(also makes a great spray-on
wax substitute).

Spray the whole ski slope and enjoy year-round skiing.

— *Hey, you can also spray down a hilly street in the summer—no need for a ski resort!*

— *You tried that once, remember, Tim?*

— *Oh yeah. That guy from the insurance company was a real jerk, wasn't he?*

99

Removes dried-on wax from chrome auto bumpers.

Avoid embarrassment: Use WD-40 to remove election bumper stickers immediately after you find out your candidate lost the election.

101

Slide oil for trombone.

— *Just make sure you have a good grip on the slide.*

— *Right, Tim: You might end up impaling someone in the string section.*

Slide oil for...

— *Watch it, Jim.*

— *Oh, yeah. Hey, you more easily amused readers: Insert your own joke here.*

**Wisdom subject to change without notice.*

Kills thistle plants.

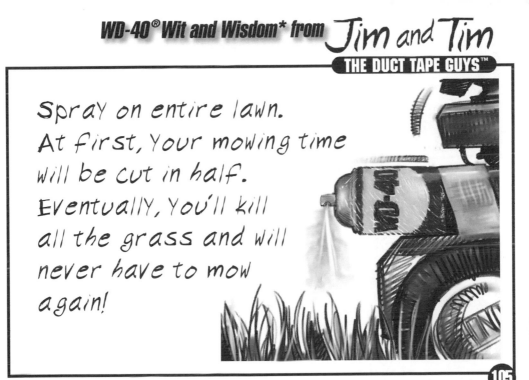

Spray on entire lawn. At first, your mowing time will be cut in half. Eventually, you'll kill all the grass and will never have to mow again!

Removes crayon and indelible marker from a variety of surfaces.

— *So, if WD-40 can remove their ink, indelible markers aren't really all that indelible.*

— *Right, Tim. They're really not indelible. They're, um... Um...*

— *Delible?*

— *Um, yeah. Delible.*

Save money! Remove crayon from coloring books when your kids are done and give them to someone else's kid.

*Wisdom subject to change without notice.

Helps untangle fishing lines.

Spray down your Christmas lights before you put them away. This will prevent tangling and save precious days when trimming next year's tree.

*Wisdom subject to change without notice.

Removes stuck
fingers from
bottles, rings, etc..

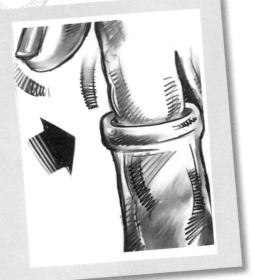

Removes arms from vending machine.

— *We wouldn't have even needed the WD-40 if you'd've just let go of that Ho-Ho.*™

— *It wasn't a Ho-Ho™ it was a Ding-Dong.*™

— *Ho-Ho™!**

— *Ding-Dong™!**

*These product endorsements come at no expense to their manufacturers. However, Jim and Tim graciously accept and encourage product compensation.

Loosens stubborn zippers.

— *Yeah, but apply in moderation to avoid unnecessary embarrassment.*

— *Yeah, and citations for indecent exposure.*

— *Shut up, Jim.*

Zippers stubborn losers.

— *What's that supposed to mean, Tim?*

— *Um, I don't know. I just...I couldn't think of anything else.*

— *Was that a crack at me?*

— *Well, if you'd come up with some more, I wouldn't have to...*

— *Just...Just zip it! We're almost done.*

Removes sticky residue from surfaces where duct tape has been removed.

— *Why would anyone remove duct tape, Jim?*

— *Why would anyone vote for Ross Perot? It's another one of life's great mysteries.*

114

Cleans up mess after You "take care" of the idiot who removed Your duct tape.

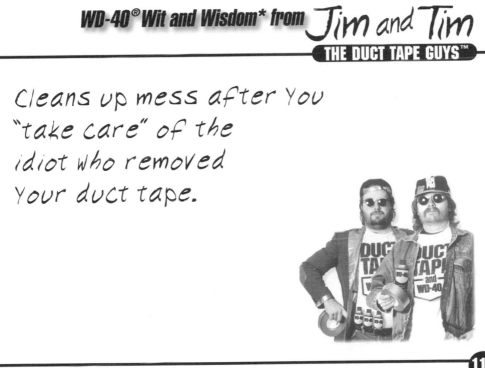

*Wisdom subject to change without notice.

Spray-Co-Matic™ Car-Care DEPLOYMENT DEVICE

WD-40

Multi-can sprayer unit fits on the grill of your car and dispenses WD-40 into the air in front of your car, resulting in:

- Less air friction—higher gas mileage.
- Fewer bugs on the grill and windshield.
- Convertible Drivers: No need for hairspray to keep hair in place.
- Prevents damage as you easily slide right off cars you hit while tailgating.
- No need to lube engine parts.
- Keeps engine cables soft and supple.
- Also perfect for wintertime driving protection: Sprays down your entire undercarriage to prevent ice, road salt, and frozen sludge build-up.

WD-40 Appendix

Unlike the human appendix, you can't just get rid of this portion of the book when you have a little side ache. WD-40 Company has received so many testimonial letters over the years, we couldn't fit them all in, so we added as many as we could fit below.*

- Cleans sticky surfaces.
- Removes dirt and grime in kitchen and bathroom.
- Removes stickers/adhesives from glass.
- Removes triple-track screens that are stuck.
- Lubricates dirty or stuck locks and latches.
- Lubricates and removes dirt and grime on sliding glass door tracks.
- Removes dirt and grease from window screens.
- Makes window shades roll easier.
- Lubricates eyeglass hinges.
- Works as a white glove finishing touch on plastic parts.

- Removes dust from artificial flowers.
- Removes starch residue from cold iron (make sure you unplug it first, of course).
- Covers scratches on glass surfaces.
- Cleans vacuum cleaner dials.
- Acts as a wood polish.
- Removes scratches from furniture.
- Removes fingerprints from surfaces.
- Waterproofs chimney for easier cleaning.
- Lubricates vertical blinds.
- Waxes floors.

*Many of the uses that appear in the appendix have not been tested by the WD-40 Company, so use them at your own risk.

- Keeps ironing boards from sticking when folded.
- Removes floodwater marks on paneling.
- Cleans hearing aid.
- Cleans plastic eyeglass lenses; removes smoked or scratched appearance.
- Untangles jewelry chains.
- Keeps wheelchair folding smoothly.
- Cleans TV remote and VCR parts.
- Lubricates wooden push-toys.
- Fixes gummed-up watch.
- Frees up barometric controls.
- Protects and cleans antiques from rust and dust.
- Fixes overwound watches.
- Takes squeaks out of recliner with coasters.
- Removes dirt and grime from sewing machines.
- Cleans and lubricates vacuum motor.

- Cleans filters in heating and air-conditioning units; makes filters more efficient and helps absorb odors.
- Shields glass from paint.
- Keeps sculptures clean and shiny.
- Removes calcium deposits in dehumidifier.
- Maintains electric shaver.
- Loosens tight Lego™ blocks.
- Removes tar from shoes.
- Removes Easter-egg dye from linoleum.
- Removes built-up mineral deposits from freezer grid.
- Removes splattered grease on Formica walls.
- Cleans silver plate and tray.
- Quiets noisy garbage disposal.
- Lubricates mixer when the beater-release won't release.
- Lubricates blade agitator assemblies in food blenders.
- Removes unwanted paint on refrigerator.

- Cleans stove.
- Cleans sink.
- Lubricates coffee grinder/frozen parts.
- Removes streaks from Formica.
- Removes stains from stainless steel sink.
- Cleans chrome fixtures in bathroom.
- Removes hard-water deposits.
- Removes soap scum from bathtub and shower.
- Frees the tank ball on the toilet.
- Takes the squeaks out of bath curtain that drags.
- Frees bathroom taps that have seized up.
- Loosens bolt on toilet seat.
- Cleans nonstick areas in bath and shower.
- Removes hardened wax from fiberglass tubs and showers.
- Cleans tile in bath and shower.

- Takes squeaks out of shoes.
- Keeps shoes shiny.
- Cleans head of cassette tape player.
- Lubricates and releases static from stereo tuner knobs.
- Unsticks keys and piano hammers.
- Lubricates record player that does not track record.
- Frees swollen storm windows after storm.
- Helps thaw outdoor faucets during winter weather.
- Lubricates louvered glass windows.
- Lubricates crank on barbeque grill.
- Prevents clothesline poles from rusting.
- Removes corrosion from the pressure switch of a water well.
- Removes dirt and grime from barbeque grill.
- Helps sharpen knives when sprayed on oil stone.
- Cleans corroded coins.

119

- Prevents concrete from sticking to inside of mixer.
- Removes graffiti.
- Cleans and polishes headstones.
- Spray on paint sprayer before painting for easier clean-up.
- Keeps dogs out of flower bed.
- Protects saw blades from rust and makes cutting easier.
- Removes dust and debris in drill holes when sprayed on drill bits.
- Cleans nozzle on spray paint can.
- Cleans varnish and beeswax off paint brush.
- Frees stuck, frozen. and/or rusted bolts.
- Lubricates screw-drive of garage door opener.
- Keeps ceramic/terra-cotta garden pots from oxidizing.
- Keeps dirt from sticking to bike or ATV (or bike and ATV driver.)
- Keeps snow from sticking to snowblowers.

- Lubricates ski boot buckles.
- Lubricates contacts and prevents rust on Christmas lights.
- Prevents snow build-up on windows.
- Keeps dirt, mud, and clay from sticking to shovels.
- Spray underside of lawn mower housing and blade to prevent sticking and clogging of grass clippings.
- Lubricates pop-up lawn sprinklers.
- Keeps wooden garden tool handles from splintering.
- Protects metal garden tools from fertilizer and garden chemicals.
- Renews typewriter, adding machine, and mechanical calculator ribbons and ink pads.
- Unsticks keyboard keys on typewriters, adding machines, and computer terminals.
- Cleans gold contact points on computers.
- Rejuvenates old computer mouse.

- Makes puck slide faster on air hockey table.
- Keeps ski boots from squeaking.
- Removes ski wax from clothing.
- Removes road tar on car.
- Removes grease and dirt on chrome.
- Helps keep paint from fading on fiberglass.
- Cleans whitewall tires.
- Helps restore paint damaged by oxidation
- Frees stuck electronic antennas and windows on cars.
- Gets air out of fuel lines when changing filters on diesel engines.
- Keeps sharpening stone clean and oiled.
- Cleans tin-plated parts on model trains.
- Dries your car's wet ignition system.
- Prevents rain seepage when sprayed on garage door sealer.
- Climbers use on crampons to keep snow from sticking.

- Keeps feathers on archery arrows water-resistant while increasing velocity and penetration.
- Jet skis/water craft: Douse whole thing in WD-40 to displace water and protect components, especially after using in salt water.
- Bicyclists use it to "blast spooge out of tight places." (Note: We have no idea what that means.)
- And finally, police have successfully used WD-40 to help them unstick and apprehend a burglar who was trapped— NAKED—in an air vent.
  (Honest! We're pretty sure the thief was stuck on the air duct's duct tape, proving once again that together, duct tape and WD-40 are keeping society safe for all of us).